MW01075943

For the Fallen, and Other Poems

FOR THE FALLEN

AND OTHER POEMS ~~ BY
LAURENCE BINYON

England mourns for her dead
across the sea."

"England mourns for her dead
across the sea."

Contents :-

FOR
THE FALLEN

"They shall grow not old, as we that are left grow old."

For the Fallen

With proud thanksgiving,
   a mother for her children,
England mourns for her dead across
   the sea.
Flesh of her flesh they were, spirit
   of her spirit,
Fallen in the cause of the free.

For the Fallen

Solemn the drums thrill : Death august
    and royal
Sings sorrow up into immortal spheres.
There is music in the midst of desolation
And a glory that shines upon our tears.

For the Fallen

They went with songs to the battle,
   they were young,
Straight of limb, true of eye, steady
   and aglow.
They were staunch to the end against
   odds uncounted,
They fell with their faces to the foe.

For the Fallen

They shall grow not old, as we that are
    left grow old:
Age shall not weary them, nor the
    years condemn.
At the going down of the sun and
    in the morning
We will remember them.

For the Fallen

They mingle not with their laughing
    comrades again;
They sit no more at familiar tables
    of home;
They have no lot in our labour of
    the day-time;
They sleep beyond England's foam.

"To the innermost heart of their own
land they are known
As the stars are known to the Night."

For the Fallen

But where our desires are and our
    hopes profound,
Felt as a well-spring that is hidden
    from sight,
To the innermost heart of their own
    land they are known
As the stars are known to the Night;

For the Fallen

As the stars that shall be bright when
we are dust,
Moving in marches upon the heavenly
plain,
As the stars that are starry in the
time of our darkness,
To the end, to the end, they remain.

THE FOURTH
OF AUGUST

"Now in thy splendour go before
us, Spirit of England."

The Fourth of August

Now in thy splendour go before us,
before us,
Spirit of England, ardent-eyed,
Enkindle this dear earth that bore us,
In the hour of peril purified.

The Fourth of August

The cares we hugged drop out of vision,
Our hearts with deeper thoughts dilate.
We step from days of sour division
Into the grandeur of our fate.

For us the glorious dead have striven,
They battled that we might be free.
We to their living cause are given;
We arm for men that are to be.

The Fourth of August

Among the nations nobliest chartered,
England recalls her heritage.
In her is that which is not bartered,
Which force can neither quell nor cage.

For her immortal stars are burning;
With her, the hope that's never done,
The seed that's in the Spring's returning,
The very flower that seeks the sun.

The Fourth of August

She fights the fraud that feeds desire on
Lies, in a lust to enslave or kill,
The barren creed of blood and iron,
Vampire of Europe's wasted will · · ·

Endure, O Earth! and thou, awaken,
Purged by this dreadful winnowing-fan,
O wronged, untameable, unshaken
Soul of divinely suffering man.

To Women

Your hearts are lifted up, your hearts
That have foreknown the utter
    price.
Your hearts burn upward like a
    flame
Of splendour and of sacrifice.

To Women

For you, you too, to battle go,

Not with the marching drums and
    cheers

But in the watch of solitude

And through the boundless night
    of fears.

To Women

Swift, swifter than those hawks of
    war,
Those threatening wings that pulse
    the air,
Far as the vanward ranks are set,
You are gone before them, you are
    there !

To Women

And not a shot comes blind
    with death

And not a stab of steel is pressed

Home, but invisibly it tore

And entered first a woman's
    breast.

"To break, but not to fail!"

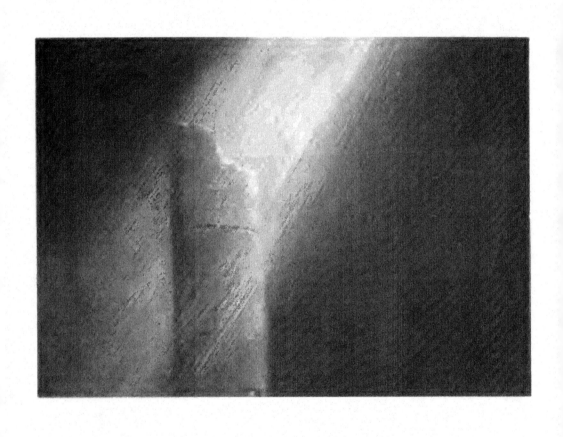

To Women

Amid the thunder of the guns,
The lightnings of the lance and
    sword
Your hope, your dread, your
    throbbing pride,
Your infinite passion is outpoured

To Women

From hearts that are as one high
   heart

Withholding naught from doom
   and bale

Burningly offered up,— to bleed,

To bear, to break, but not to fail !

CPSIA information can be obtained
at www.ICGtesting.com
Printed in the USA
LVOW13*0911130518

577034LV00013B/146/P